Chic & Unique
flower arrangements

Chic & Unique

flower arrangements

Over 35 modern
designs for
simple floral
table decorations

Julie Collins & Tina Parkes
Academy of Floral Art

D&C
David and Charles

CONTENTS

Introduction

When asked to write an introduction for this book, the first thing we did was to put on our boots, grab the dog and go for a walk to gather some inspiration. This represents the essence of what this book is about: being inspired by the things around you, freeing your creativity and having lots of fun making the designs – either for your home, for a special event, or with a group of friends.

Together we have created an innovative internationally recognized floral design and floristry school called the Academy of Floral Art. In this school we offer enthusiasts several courses that range from the prestigious British City & Guilds Master Diploma in Professional Floristry Level 5 through to our fun and inspirational recreational floral design courses.

The Academy of Floral Art is represented on the British Floristry Association Education Board, and this year we have been nominated as one of the top floristry colleges in the UK. We are truly passionate about creating excellence in floral design and floristry, as well as inspiring a new generation of floral designers to continue this beautiful tradition.

The designs

We have created a range of beautiful designs for this book and we hope these will inspire you to try them out for yourselves. In creating this collection, it was important that the designs were romantic, pretty and soft; it was also important that the designs were easy to recreate without using an abundance of floral material, thus keeping your costs as low as possible.

We love discovering materials while on walks or in the garden that can be used in our designs. We would encourage you to source similar local materials whenever possible although, at the same time, all the designs can be made with artificial flowers and foliage. We would also like to encourage you to be flexible; if you can't get hold of the flower or container shown, simply adapt the design to work with what you do have.

The team

As well as creating our own designs for the collection, we invited three other floral designers to join our team to add diversity and style to the collection:

Donna Cann and **Amanda Randell** are two of our top students, who have just completed with us the prestigious City & Guilds Master Diploma in Professional Floristry, and they have been able to contribute considerable flair and originality to their designs.

Catherine Date, who has taught for us on a freelance basis and holds a National Diploma of the Society of Floristry, has been inspirational, as her experience in wedding and competition design brings a strong commercial element to her beautiful work.

The five designers working on this book were presented with six areas of inspiration to work with, as follows:

Theme 1: The beach
Theme 2: Garden wedding
Theme 3: Hotel
Theme 4: Marquee
Theme 5: Country house
Theme 6: Eco-friendly

If you are looking for further inspiration we have a DVD that accompanies this book, which shows a range of designs and some of the techniques we have used; it is available from our website. Maybe one day we will even have the opportunity to meet you on one of our courses, again available for purchase from our website.

For whatever occasion you are creating your designs – for a wedding, entertaining or simply to decorate your home – we do hope you will enjoy making the designs as much as we have. We would love to see your interpretations, so please send us a picture on Facebook and we may even put it on our website.

Website: www.academyoffloralart.com
Facebook: www.facebook.com/pages/Academy-of-Floral-Art

Julie Collins and Tina Parkes

LEVEL 1

LEVEL 2

LEVEL 3

How to Use this Book

We have designed this book like a course in Levels, each one representing an increased level of experience. If you work consistently through Levels 1 to 3 you will expand your knowledge; alternatively, if you would like to dip in and out of the projects you will be able to quickly find a design suitable for your level of expertize.

If you are a novice, you may like to start at the beginning and build up your skills as you work through. On the other hand, if a design catches your eye and inspires you, then that might also be the perfect place to start.

LEVEL 1: These designs are excellent for a beginner to try, as no experience is required. Many use limited flower material, which can help to keep your costs down. Sometimes the simplest things are the best!

LEVEL 2: These designs are little more advanced and use more techniques, making them ideal for those with some experience of working with flowers. Essentially, these designs need a little more understanding with the placement of the flowers.

LEVEL 3: Experience is essential for these more advanced designs. They are more challenging and often take longer to make owing to the intricate techniques used. These are ideal for those who love to explore the possibilities of construction in floral design and we hope they may inspire you to create your own versions.

Our flower recipes

We have styled the book like a recipe book. So along with the essential floristry techniques that are explained at the end of the book, each design has:

- A list of flower, foliage and sundry ingredients to gather for making up the design.
- Symbols to indicate the approximate time it will take to complete each project and whether the design can be made with fresh or artificial alternatives, e.g:

fresh   artificial

approx. 20 mins

- A recipe that explains with clear instructions and step photos exactly how to assemble the design.
- Make It Chic and Make It Unique tips that offer suggestions to bring a little extra flair to your design.

Flower names

Where the common name is widely recognized, we have used this for the flower e.g. rose. Otherwise we have used the Latin names, with their common alternatives where appropriate, presenting them all in lower case in order to make them easier to read.

Getting Started

Selecting the location

Before starting a design, it is always best to consider the location in which it will be displayed. This includes the setting, the surface on which the design will sit, and the colourways and theme of the room decoration. You may also need to measure the space available to establish the best size for the arrangement.

This pretty posy design is in a square container, so it would sit perfectly on a square or rectangular table. Being soft and romantic, it would make the perfect design for a pink-themed wedding table.

This design has a festive feel and is best suited to a long dining table, lending itself to being repeated at intervals along the surface. Being very low, it will not restrict the view of guests.

Gathering your materials

We recommend that you source your container first so that you can gauge the amount of flowers and foliage you will need to fill it. Containers can be sourced from a variety of places such as garden centres, florist and charity stores and recycling centres; in some designs we have even shown you how to make your own. Before you start work, do ensure that your container is clean and waterproof.

Once your container is chosen, gather together all the additional equipment you will need for the design, as listed in each project. Specialist floristry materials can be purchased from your local florist or from an online floristry supplier. Again, do ensure that scissors and knives are clean and sharp before you start to work with them.

When it comes to buying your flowers, freshness is important. We recommend ordering the flowers a week in advance from your florist or supplier, then collecting them two days prior to making the design. This will allow time to condition the flowers to ensure longevity. Using seasonal flowers is another method by which to secure longevity.

Cutting and picking

Cutting foliage and flowers from your own garden creates a very personal design and can also help reduce the cost of materials. Here are some tips on cutting and picking your own flowers (see also Preparing Flowers and Foliage):

- Always use clean tools to avoid bacteria being passed into the stem; this will reduce the life span of both the cut material and the parent plant.

- Always use sharp tools to ensure a clean cut. Use secateurs to cut woody or thick stems; use scissors for finer, delicate or hollow stems.

- Always cut the stem at an angle to ensure the flower or foliage can take up water; if you cut the stem straight across it will sit flat against the bottom of the container, thus reducing the stem's ability to take up water.

- When cutting, take along a clean bucket of water into which you can put the flowers straightaway; this will help to extend their vase life.

- Cut garden materials in the morning but not after a heavy shower or dew; some flowers and leaves will mark or rot if water is left on them.

- Cut flowers in bud, when you can begin to see some colour.

- Cut only materials that are in good condition with no evidence of pests or diseases, as these will quickly spread to your other flowers.

- Place cut flowers and foliage in water in a cool, dark place for at least two to three hours before working with them to allow them a good drink.

- Before arranging, remove excess foliage above and all foliage below the water line; this will extend the life of the materials.

In this level we introduce simple yet effective designs. The key to success for these is keeping your work neat and tidy.

Candle Magic

The warm colours and textures of roses and fruit combine in a rich, classic design that is easy to make. The white candle adds strong contrast, creating a stunning centrepiece or decoration that is perfect for any special occasion.

DESIGNED BY JULIE COLLINS

Ingredients

Flowers
- 10 red roses (A)
- 2 clematis or ivy vines (B)
- 5 nectarines or red apples
- 5 peaches
- 10 cherries
- 1 small bunch of green grapes
- 1 box of redcurrants

Sundries
- 1 candle
- 1 flat and edged cake stand or bowl

Optional extra
- 10 glass test tubes

Recipe

1. First place the candle in the centre of the cake stand or bowl.

2. Arrange a selection of nectarines (or red apples) and peaches around the candle, stacking the occasional fruit to create a slightly raised effect.

3. Continue placing the fruit evenly around the bowl, filling in the gaps between the pieces with grapes and cherries, then drape the redcurrants over the stacked fruit.

4. Add the roses, either placed so that the stems reach the bottom of the bowl or place in test tubes filled with water.

5. Drape and tuck in the clematis or ivy vines and add approximately 2cm (¾in) of water to the bowl.

6. Mist spray the arrangement to finish.

{ **make it unique** }
Bring a period feel to your design by displaying it on top of a doily

LEVEL 1  fresh or artificial approx. 20 mins

Modern Simplicity

Contemporary gerberas contrast strikingly with a simple metal dish to create clean shapes in this modern design. It will make the perfect decoration to add a touch of style to any table top.

DESIGNED BY DONNA CANN

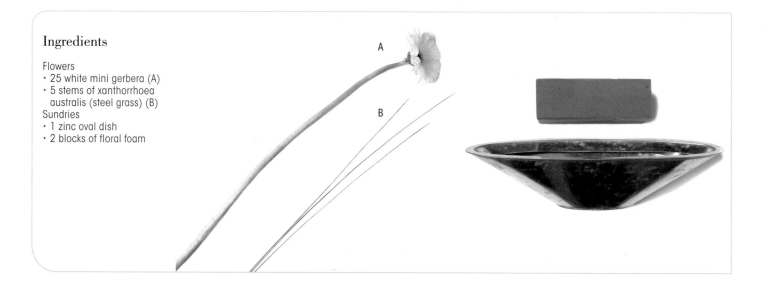

Ingredients

Flowers
- 25 white mini gerbera (A)
- 5 stems of xanthorrhoea australis (steel grass) (B)

Sundries
- 1 zinc oval dish
- 2 blocks of floral foam

Recipe

1. Soak the floral foam (see Techniques), then place it in the oval dish so that it sits 3cm (1in) above the rim.

2. Cut the gerbera stems and place the flower heads in neat rows that follow along the contours of the dish.

3. Measure the five stems of steel grass to the length of the dish, then snap them at 90-degree angles to create a rectangular frame that will sit above the design.

4. Place the five stems over the top of the design in lines that are parallel to each other. Push the angled ends of the stems gently into the foam to ensure that they stay in position.

{ **make it unique**
Keep the gerbera heads in very straight lines to bring the most impact to your design. }

Linking the Line

This elegant design uses gentle loops of flexi grass to link the bold, upright shapes of the agapanthus flowers into a precise line. The arrangement has a unique architectural quality that will become the centre of attention.

DESIGNED BY AMANDA RANDELL

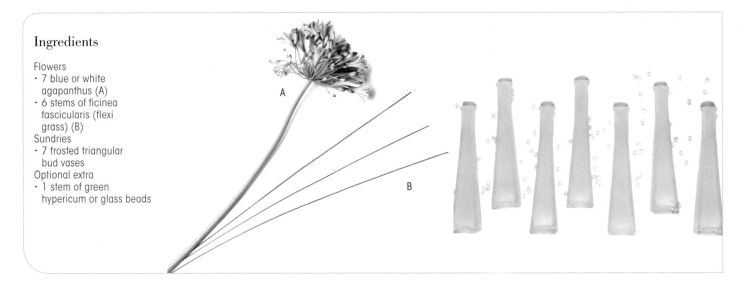

Ingredients

Flowers
- 7 blue or white agapanthus (A)
- 6 stems of ficinea fascicularis (flexi grass) (B)

Sundries
- 7 frosted triangular bud vases

Optional extra
- 1 stem of green hypericum or glass beads

Recipe

1. First fill the seven triangular bud vases with water.

2. Lay out the vases in a straight line with equal spacing between each one, using a measure to ensure they are evenly spaced. It is important to arrange this design in the position in which it will be displayed as it cannot be moved once it has been made.

3. Cut all the agapanthus stems to the same height, so the head of each flower reaches to approximately three times the height of the container, then place one stem in each container.

4. Loop each strand of flexi grass between two vases to link them. Ensure that the top of each loop reaches the same height to create a consistent effect.

{ **make it unique** }
Thread some green hypericum berries or add glass beads onto the flexi grass to embellish your design.

18

LEVEL 1   fresh or artificial   approx. 15 mins

Round and Wound

This is a flower arrangement with a difference, where the containers create the primary shapes and the bright flowers embellish these with vibrant highlights.

DESIGNED BY AMANDA RANDELL

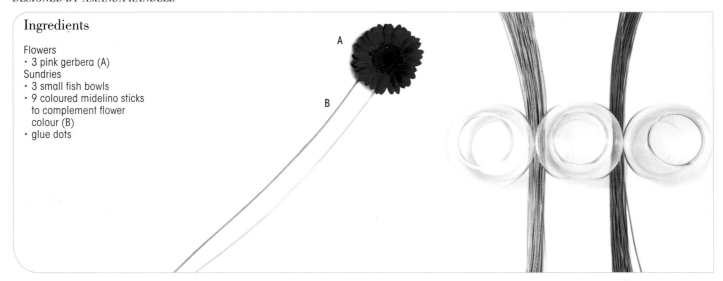

Ingredients

Flowers
- 3 pink gerbera (A)

Sundries
- 3 small fish bowls
- 9 coloured midelino sticks to complement flower colour (B)
- glue dots

Recipe

1. In the position in which the design will be displayed, first fill each of the three fish bowls about one-third full with water.

2. Now curve three midelino sticks in contrasting colours gently around the inside of each fish bowl.

3. Cut the stems from the flowers and float a flower head in each bowl.

4. Gently place the bowls on top of each other, making sure they are well balanced. If necessary, secure each vase in position with a few glue dots.

{ **make it chic**
Instead of gerbera, try using cymbidium orchid heads or tulips for an elegant twist on this original design. }

LEVEL 1  fresh or artificial approx. 20 mins

Pretty Pail

This romantic design juxtaposes a soft, feminine palette and delicate chiffon ribbon with a decorated metal bucket (pail) for instant shabby chic appeal.

DESIGNED BY JULIE COLLINS

Ingredients

Flowers
- 10 small pink roses (A)
- 1 mini gerbera (B)
- 5 white dianthus barbatus (sweet william) (C)
- 10 malus (crab apples) (D)

Sundries
- block floral foam
- 1 bucket (pail)
- 1m (1yd) chiffon ribbon
- pot tape
- 10 cocktail sticks (toothpicks)

Recipe

1. Soak the floral foam (see Techniques). Shape it to fit the pail, securing with pot tape.

2. Cut all the flower stems approximately 7cm (2¾in) long then cover the foam with sweet william.

3. Place the single gerbera slightly off-centre and evenly place the roses around the design, thus creating a slightly domed profile.

4. Inset a cocktail stick into the bottom of each crab apple. Push them into the foam so they are evenly placed around the arrangement.

5. Make a bow from the chiffon ribbon and tie it onto the pail handle.

6. Mist spray the arrangement to finish.

{ **make it unique** }
Stencil your own design onto a vintage pail using a homemade or shop-bought stencil.

LEVEL 1   fresh or artificial   approx. 30 mins

1

Crisscross Callas

This effective design uses just a few choice flowers to make a chic addition to a wedding table. As seasonal alternatives to callas lilies, try using tulips or bluebells in the spring or clematis in the summer.

DESIGNED BY AMANDA RANDELL

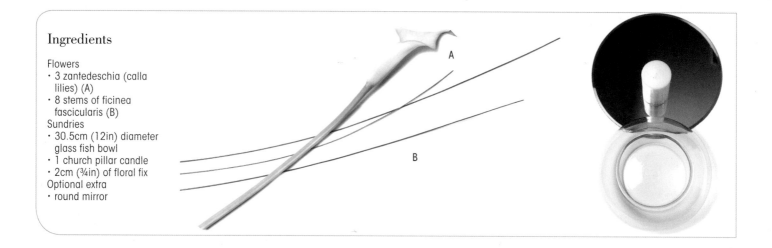

Ingredients

Flowers
- 3 zantedeschia (calla lilies) (A)
- 8 stems of ficinea fascicularis (B)

Sundries
- 30.5cm (12in) diameter glass fish bowl
- 1 church pillar candle
- 2cm (¾in) of floral fix

Optional extra
- round mirror

Recipe

1. Clean the fish bowl, then take the eight stems of flexi grass and wind them around the inside, ensuring that the end of each stem is in contact with the bottom of the bowl.

2. Take the first calla lily and gently warm the stem with your hand, then curve it over your thumb.

3. If the stems are very firm, take a sharp knife and peel off a thin line from the head of the stem to the base, which will help make it more flexible.

4. Wind the stem around the inside of the bowl, again making sure the stem touches the bottom of the bowl. Repeat this process with the further two stems, crossing them over at different points to create a pleasing crisscross design.

5. Finally add the candle through the centre of the stems, securing it to the bottom of the bowl using floral fix, then add a small amount of water to the bowl to allow the flowers and grasses to drink.

make it chic

{ *Try displaying the design on a round mirror; this will enhance the lighting of the design and reflect the crisscross shapes of the grass.* }

LEVEL 1   fresh or artificial ⏱ approx. 30 mins

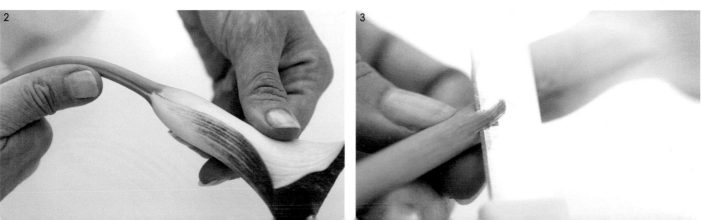

Floral Cupcakes

This glorious design uses a warm pink colour combination and flower heads resting in cupcake cases – interspersed with edible cupcakes – to add a touch of vintage chic to any afternoon teatime display.

DESIGNED BY CATHERINE DATE

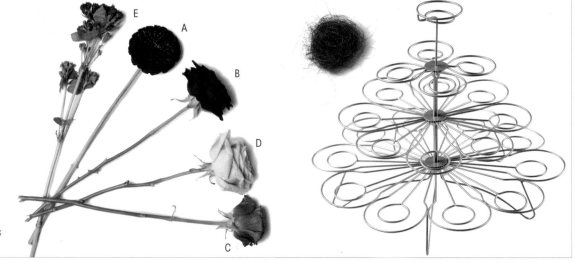

Ingredients

Flowers
- 3 red dahlia (A)
- 2 red roses (B)
- 3 dark pink roses (C)
- 3 light pink roses (D)
- 2 cerise bouvardia (E)
- 1 box of strawberries

Sundries
- 13 to 15 cupcake cases
- edible cupcakes to mix into the display
- cupcake stand
- clear glue
- a handful of sisal

Optional extra
- antique cups and saucers

Recipe

1. Cut off each flower just below its head. To help seal the stems, add a small amount of glue to the cut edge of the flower head and allow this to dry.

2. Rest a single flower head in each cupcake case; if needed, place a little sisal around the flower to help support the head in an upright position.

3. To display, layer your floral cupcakes around your stand along with some edible cupcakes and strawberries.

{ **make it chic**
To develop this vintage chic look, perhaps for a wedding, try incorporating flower heads into a selection of antique cups and saucers. }

LEVEL 1    fresh or artificial approx. 40 mins

Orchid Rock Pool

In this beautifully simple seaside design the glass effectively magnifies the orchid flowers, providing the arrangement with strong lines and immediate impact.

DESIGNED BY AMANDA RANDELL

Ingredients

Flowers
- 1 stem of cymbidium orchids (A)

Sundries
- 2 cylinder vases of different sizes
- clean sand
- shells and pebbles
- 7 floating candles
- fine fishing line or craft nylon thread
- small weights or stones

A

Recipe

1. First ensure that the vases and sand are completely clean, then fill the vases with water. Add a layer of sand to the bottom of each and allow it to settle, then place a selection of shells on top of the sand.

2. You can either anchor the orchids so they rest among the shells or float them two-thirds of the way up the vase. To do either, first cut the heads from the flowers and tie the fishing line around their stems.

3. Add a weight to the end of the line at the desired length then carefully drop the flower heads into the water. Bury the weights in the sand so they can't be seen, then float the candles on top.

4. Place the design in situ; you will need to allow for the design to settle and the water to clear before it is completely finished.

make it unique

To alter the design, try using coloured sand or gravel instead of plain sand. Wash it before you start, as this will prevent it from clouding the water.

LEVEL 1   fresh or artificial   approx. 20 mins

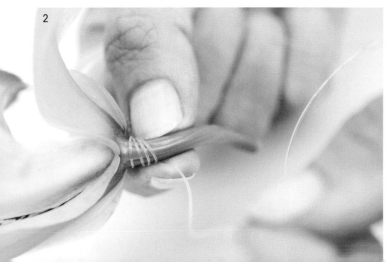

On the Beach

Reminiscent of sandy beaches and the enjoyment these can bring, this design is ideal for a beach-themed party or wedding. Even better, the minimal flower use makes the design quick-to-make and cost-effective.

DESIGNED BY JULIE COLLINS

Ingredients

Flowers
- 3 blue agapanthus (A)
- 5 white nigella (B)

Sundries
- 1 glass cube vase
- clean sand
- shells
- rope
- ⅓ block of floral foam
- funnel
- glue dot

Recipe

1. Cut the floral foam so it fits easily inside the glass cube vase, allowing for space around each side and over the top of the foam for the sand.

2. Soak the floral foam (see Techniques) and place it in the vase, then fill around its edges with sand using a funnel. The sand should nearly reach the top of the block. Try not to get any on the top itself at this stage as this can make inserting the flowers harder.

3. With the foam firmly wedged in place by the sand, add an agapanthus. To do this, measure the stem against the vase to determine how high you want the finished design to be, then cut the stem and push into the foam.

4. Add the second agapanthus stem to reach just a little lower than the first, then add the third, which should reach about halfway up the length of the design. Fill in around the agapanthus with nigella.

5. Add a little more sand to completely cover the top of the foam, then decorate the top with shells. Twist rope around the outside of the vase and secure with a glue dot to complete.

{ **make it unique**
Use coloured sand to alter the look of this design. }

LEVEL 1  fresh or artificial approx. 30 mins

Little Pots

Fill pretty little vases with summer flowers and perhaps even grasses to create this soft, wild flower design. These handy vases are purchased already attached together, making them ideal to quickly place on a wedding table or anywhere that requires a touch of country charm.

DESIGNED BY AMANDA RANDELL

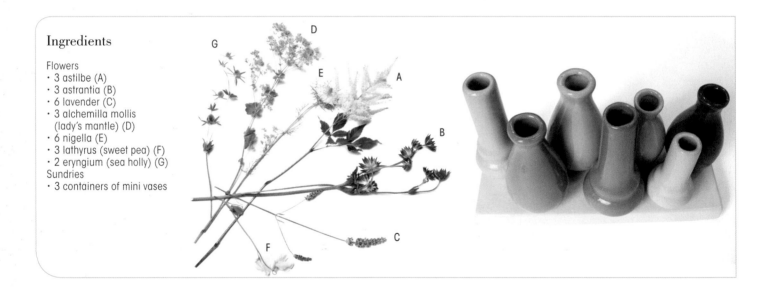

Ingredients

Flowers
· 3 astilbe (A)
· 3 astrantia (B)
· 6 lavender (C)
· 3 alchemilla mollis (lady's mantle) (D)
· 6 nigella (E)
· 3 lathyrus (sweet pea) (F)
· 2 eryngium (sea holly) (G)
Sundries
· 3 containers of mini vases

Recipe

1. Start by ensuring that the flower material you choose for the design is well conditioned, as these mini vases only hold a small amount of water. When your flowers are ready to be cut, fill the vases with water.

2. Remove any leaves from the stems of the flowers that will fit inside in the vases. This will make them easier to place and will keep the water fresher for longer.

3. Cut the stems of your flowers to the appropriate length and then start to position them in your vases. Try to use just one flower material in each vase to achieve a simple, clean look.

{ make it chic }
Create a more compact design by positioning the three containers of mini vases in a square shape on a decorative platter.

32

LEVEL 1 ✿✿ fresh or artificial ⏱ approx. 10 mins for each pot

Vintage Vase

Here is a classic design that will complement any setting. An
aspidistra leaf and a white ribbon tied around the vase add an extra
decorative quality to soften the arrangement and hide the stems.

DESIGNED BY JULIE COLLINS

Ingredients

Flowers
- 3 white eustoma
  (lisianthus) (A)
- 3 white bouvardia (B)
- 6 white mini gerbera (C)
- 4 white roses (D)
- 6 alchemilla mollis
  (lady's mantle) (E)
- 10 stems of panicum
  virgatum (fountain
  grass) (F)
- 1 aspidistra leaf (G)
- 5 stems of eucalyptus
  pulverulenta 'baby blue' (H)

Sundries
- 1 glass vase
- 1m (1yd) of ribbon
- glue dots

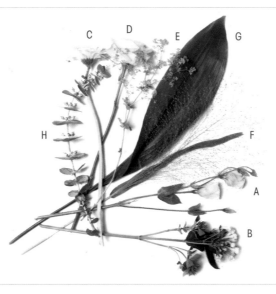

Recipe

1. Clean the vase and fill halfway with water. Include flower food so the blooms last longer and the water remains as clean as possible.

2. First add all the stems of eucalyptus and five stems of the fountain grass; this creates your basic structure and will help support the flower stems.

3. Now place the best rose in the centre of the foliage and vase. At a slightly lower height, add three further roses around this central flower.

4. Cut to a lower height again, add three mini gerbera between the roses and fill in with some of the lady's mantle. In the gaps, add the bouvardia and lisianthus followed by the last three gerbera.

5. Finally, add the last of the lady's mantle and fountain grasses to flow out of the design and fill any remaining gaps.

6. To finish, wrap the aspidistra leaf around the vase and secure in place with a glue dot. Finally, add a tied ribbon to soften the design.

make it chic

*When creating a classic floral
arrangement, the central flower will
dictate the height of the design.
Generally, the vase should measure
between a half and one-third of the
total height of the tallest flower.*

LEVEL 1   fresh or artificial   approx. 40 mins

In this level we try some new techniques, particularly exploring the placement of flowers so they are pleasing to the eye.

Floating Grasses

This ethereal arrangement uses grasses to freshen and soften any interior setting. The flower here is triteleia, a native to western USA and particularly common in California, whose name is derived from tri (meaning 'three', as the flower part comes in threes) and teleios (meaning 'perfect').

DESIGNED BY AMANDA RANDELL

Ingredients

Flowers
· 20 triteleia (brodia) (A)
· 20 stems of
  panicum virgatum
  (fountain grass) (B)
Sundries
· 1 glass jug
· string or raffia

Recipe

1. First lay the flowers and grasses out on your work surface, being careful to handle the grasses very gently as they have very fine stems and break easily. To start building your bouquet, pick up three or four stems of fountain grass at the point that will be approximately halfway down the jug (see Spiralling Stems).

2. Add a couple of stems of the brodia, keeping the stems straight, then add more of the grasses and brodia, starting to spiral the stems around the first ones. Keep alternating the material until you are holding it all in your hand.

3. Very gently twist the stems in the direction of the spiral, which will help splay the flower and grass heads out.

4. Tie the bunch at the point you are holding them with string or raffia, then cut the stems so the bouquet will fit into the jug.

{ **make it unique** }
Plenty of summer flowers work really well in this design; you could try using centaurea cyanus (cornflower) and dianthus (pinks).

LEVEL 2   fresh   approx. 20 mins

Hazel Twists

Contorted hazel twigs make a wonderful structure on which to display these gorgeous purple orchid heads. Together, they combine to make a chic, minimalist alternative to the more traditional, abundant flower design.

DESIGNED BY AMANDA RANDELL

Ingredients

Flowers
- 1 bundle of contorted hazel twigs (A)
- 1 stem of vanda orchid (B)

Sundries
- 1m (1yd) of velvet ribbon
- 1 tub of glass crystals
- 1 tall cylindrical vase
- glue dots
- clear glue

Recipe

1. Gently place a layer of glass crystals into the bottom of the vase.

2. Wind the length of ribbon around the bottom of the vase and secure it in position with a glue dot.

3. Wedge the hazel twigs into the glass crystals at the base of the vase until they are stable.

4. Now cut the orchid heads and seal the stem at the bottom of each flower head with glue so the design lasts longer.

5. When the glue has become tacky rather than wet, stick the orchid heads to the hazel twigs, starting from the inside of the vase then working up to the top. Try to group the heads to create more impact.

{ **make it unique** }
This design fully lends itself to being made with artificial materials.

LEVEL 2   fresh or artificial ⏱ approx. 30 mins

Country Basket

This soft, romantic design uses a hat-shaped basket and a palette of pastel shades to evoke a dreamy rustic backdrop of flower-filled meadows and times gone by.

DESIGNED BY JULIE COLLINS

Ingredients

Flowers
- 3 stems of eucalyptus pulverulenta 'baby blue' (A)
- 2 purple astrantia (B)
- 5 white nigella (C)
- 5 white roses (D)
- 2 eryngium (sea holly) (E)

Sundries
- 1 hat-shaped basket
- ¼ block of floral foam
- 1 floral frog
- floral fix
- handful of burgundy sisal

Recipe

1. Make sure the basket container is waterproof and dry. Using floral fix, attach the floral frog to the base of the container.

2. Soak the floral foam (see Techniques) then place it firmly on top of the frog, ensuring that it is securely in place.

3. Gently tease out the sisal to create a fine layer of material, then place this across the top of the foam and basket to provide the design with contrasting texture under the flowers.

4. Cover the foam with short pieces of the eucalyptus stems, arranging them so that they radiate out from the centre.

5. Finish by inserting the rose, astrantia, sea holly and nigella flowers into the foam. Start by placing a rose in the centre, then evenly position the other flowers around it to create a shallow dome shape.

{ **make it unique** }
Try adding a layer of sisal on top of the design to create a romantic veil.

LEVEL 2   fresh or artificial   approx. 30 mins

By the Sea

A gorgeous design reminiscent of long summer days spent by the coast. The rich hues of the blue scabiosa and purple veronica perfectly encapsulate the brilliant blues of the sky and sea, and the pebbles further enhance the seaside theme.

DESIGNED BY CATHERINE DATE

Ingredients

Flowers
- 5 blue scabiosa (A)
- 2 tanacetum (feverfew) (B)
- 5 purple veronica (C)
- 2 white nigella (D)
- 10 small aspidistra leaves (E)

Sundries
- 10 plastic test tubes
- lilac bullion wire
- elastic band
- glue dots
- white pebbles
- grey plate

Optional extra
- 10 stems of picked grasses (F)

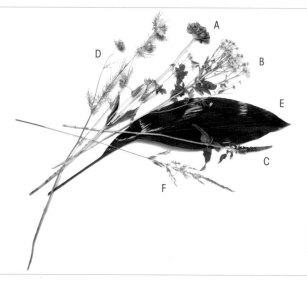

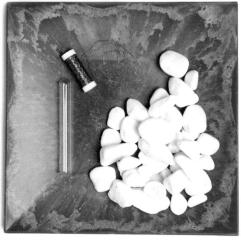

Recipe

1. First gently roll the test tubes in the soft parts of the aspidistra leaves to cover the outside surfaces.

2. Once covered, cut the leaves and secure with a glue dot.

3. Then bind bullion wire around each leaf and tube to secure the leaf and to add decorative detail.

4. When all ten test tubes are covere

1

2

LEVEL 2  fresh or artificial approx. 40 mins

temporarily secure them together with an elastic band. Using more bullion wire, wrap around all the test tubes to secure together and form a container that will stand freely. Remove the elastic band when the container is secure.

5. Now fill the test tubes with water and cut the flowers to different lengths.

6. Add the flowers to the test tubes to create a vegetative, layered design. Start with the tallest stem and work down to the shortest to create visual balance.

7. To finish, place the container in the centre of the plate and arrange pebbles around its base.

{ **make it unique**
For a quick alternative, recycle an old tin can. Wrap an aspidistra leaf around the tin can and secure it with bullion wire, then insert soaked foam below the rim of the container. }

Sunny Meadow

This rustic design recreates sunny fields filled to the brim with bold, bright sunflowers, ideal for adding a happy, summery touch to any table top – indoors or out.

DESIGNED BY JULIE COLLINS

Ingredients

Flowers
- 4 or 5 helianthus (sunflowers) (A)
- 5 large leaves e.g. acer, virginia creeper or ivy (B)
- 1 bundle of straw

Sundries
- 50cm (20in) length of cellophane
- sticky tape
- ½ block of floral foam
- 2m (2yd) of brown wool

Recipe

1. Soak the floral foam (see Techniques) and then place it in the centre of your piece of cellophane.

2. Wrap the cellophane around the foam like a parcel, leaving the top open (see Techniques). Then cut the cellophane level with the foam so that the top of the block remains uncovered.

3. Stretch the length of wool in a line on the table and spread out the straw along it (see Techniques). Put the foam on its side and place it on top of the straw, then pick up the wool and draw the straw around the foam. Tie the ends of the wool, then wrap the remaining length around the design several times. Neaten the effect by trimming the straw as required.

4. Arrange the leaves around the edge of the foam so they overlap the straw.

5. To complete the design, cut the sunflower stems short and insert them into the foam. Finally, infill any remaining gaps with large leaves.

LEVEL 2   fresh or artificial   approx. 20 mins

Fields of Gold

This nature-inspired design evokes those lazy, late-summer days when
the wheat ripens and meadow flowers are blooming in abundance.

DESIGNED BY TINA PARKES

Ingredients

Flowers
- 1 bunch centaurea
  (cornflower) (A)
- 1 bunch triticum
  (wheat) (B)
- 5 thlaspi (C)
- 2 tanacetum
  (feverfew) (D)
- 1 mahonia seed head (E)

Sundries
- 1 glass cube vase
- ⅓ block floral foam

LEVEL 2   🌸🌸 fresh or artificial   ⏱ approx. 40 mins

Recipe

1. Soak the floral foam (see Techniques) and cut it so that it sits in the vase leaving a 1cm (⅜in) gap all around the edge. Ensure the foam is level with the top of the vase.

2. Place three-quarters of the wheat on the work surface and cut all the stems to the same length.

3. Insert the wheat between the floral foam and the container, until all the foam is concealed.

4. Place the remaining wheat in the centre of the design and arrange the flowers between the wheat.

5. Loop the mahonia seed head stems around the edge of the design. This will create a rough circular frame when viewed from overhead.

{ make it chic }
This design looks best when the cornflowers are fully open.

Flower Sushi

Bring a taste of the contemporary Orient to your flower arranging by trying your hand at this fun and effective flower sushi. Play around with colours and textures until you achieve the ultimate mouth-watering design.

DESIGNED BY DONNA CANN

Ingredients

Flowers
- 3 white chrysanthemum (A)
- 3 eryngium (sea holly) (B)
- 2 green hydrangea (C)

Sundries
- slate-coloured plastic square container
- 1 block of floral foam
- slate pieces
- 2m (2yd) of waterproof grey ribbon
- 4 to 6 floral frogs
- 4cm (1½in) of floral fix

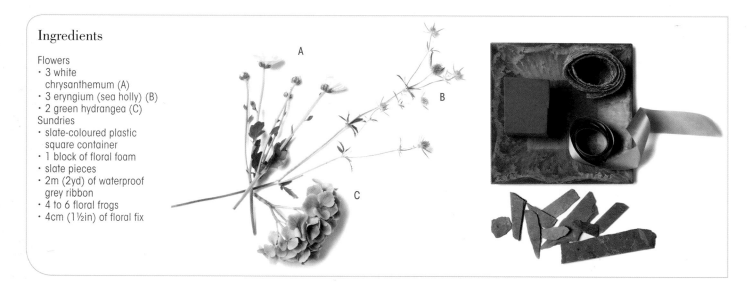

LEVEL 2   fresh or artificial   approx. 1 hour

3 4

Recipe

1. Cut the floral foam block in half lengthways to create two shallow slabs of foam, then soak (see Techniques). Attach floral fix to the frogs, secure them evenly to the base of the container, then place the foam on top to create a square.

2. Lightly mark the surface of the foam to divide it into sushi-shaped sections. Lay a head from each type of flower in each of the sections, moving them around until you are happy with the pattern.

3. Start to push the slate pieces into the foam to clearly define the sections.

4. Continue to build up the slate dividers in the same way.

5. Pin the grey ribbon around the outside edge of the foam to help contain the design and to hold the two pieces of foam together.

6. To finish, cut the flowers short and add them to the design by pushing them securely into the foam. Ensure you do this neatly and evenly, one section at a time.

{ make it chic }

Contrasting colours and textures, will give this design more impact.

Hazy Days

This gorgeously rustic design combines meadow flowers and hay to evoke hazy summer fields. The addition of grasses to the posy design provides it with height and movement to enhance this meadow feel.

DESIGNED BY JULIE COLLINS

Ingredients

Flowers
- 10 tanacetum (feverfew) (A)
- 5 alchemilla mollis (lady's mantle) (B)
- 12 stems of meadow grass

Sundries
- ½ block of floral foam
- 50cm (20in) of cellophane
- sticky tape
- a handful of straw
- 1m (1yd) of string
- 2m (2yd) of raffia

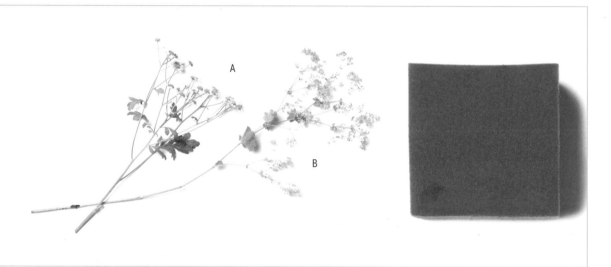

Recipe

1. Wrap the cellophane around the floral foam block (see Techniques) leaving the top open, then use sticky tape to fix the cellophane in place.

2. Lay a length of string on a table, then tease out a layer of straw along the top of the string. Place the wrapped foam in the centre of the straw and, using either ends of the string, pull the straw up around the foam.

3. When all the edges of the foam are covered, secure the straw around it by tying the string ends together. Tightly bind the raffia over the string to cover it, creating a decorative feature.

4. Cut the lady's mantle and the feverfew flowers quite short and push them into the foam to create a posy shape. Once the foam is covered with flowers, add your grasses. Cut the grasses taller than the flowers to provide movement to the arrangement.

5. Mist spray the arrangement to finish.

{ **make it unique** }
Daisies will add a cottage garden or vintage flavour to any design you create.

LEVEL 2  fresh or artificial approx. 45 mins

Pretty in Pink

To achieve the rich effect of this pretty pink posy, it is important to choose flowers with a good range of textures and shapes.

DESIGNED BY CATHERINE DATE

Ingredients

Flowers
- 7 pink roses (A)
- 5 plum-coloured dahlia (B)
- 5 pink bouvardia (C)
- 10 large leaves e.g. bergenia (D), aspidistra or ivy
- 2 lilac hydrangea (E)
- 2 pink astrantia (F)
- 2 pink eustoma (lisianthus) (G)
- 6 galax leaves (H)

Sundries
- 1 block of floral foam
- 1 square pink ceramic container
- purple bullion wire

LEVEL 2   fresh or artificial   approx. 45 mins

Recipe

1. Cut the floral foam to fit the container. If possible, cover the entire base with a deep layer of foam to make it easier to position the flowers that have shorter stems.

2. Roll the large leaves and secure with a couple of staples.

3. Decorate the rolled leaves with purple bullion wire.

4. Position the roses in the foam in groups of two or three; these become the focal flowers. Similarly, add the dahlia in groups of two or three, then insert the stems of the rolled leaves into the foam, some singly and some in groups of two.

5. Add groups of bouvardia and lisianthus to reach a slightly lower height than the other flowers; this adds more texture to the arrangement.

6. Fill in the remaining gaps with hydrangea, astrantia and galax leaves, then mist spray the design to help it to last.

{ **make it chic** }
To add a romantic touch, add some loops of chiffon ribbon.

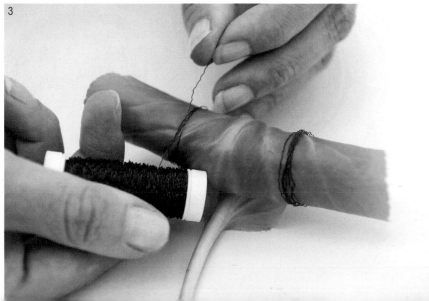

Flowers in a Teacup

This mixture of flowers and leaves arranged in a teacup creates a trendy, vintage design. Wicker teacups are available as well as china, and you could also pick up smaller china sets at thrift stores for a very reasonable price.

DESIGNED BY TINA PARKES

Ingredients

Flowers
- 4 deep pink roses (A)
- 1 cream spray rose (B)
- 2 pink astrantia (C)
- 5 itea virginica (D)
- 2 leycesteria (pheasant berry) (E)
- 2 trails of clematis (F)
- 6 heuchera leaves (G)
- a handful of tillandsia moss (H)

Sundries
- 1 large china teacup and saucer
- 1 plastic dish that reaches halfway up inside the cup,
- 1/3 block of floral foam
- 1m (1yd) of wire-edged ribbon, light coffee colour
- pot tape
- 2 to 3cm (¾ to 1¼in) of floral fix

Recipe

1. Cut the floral foam to fit the plastic dish; in height the foam should reach about 2 to 3cm (¾ to 1¼in) above the rim of the teacup. With a knife, slightly curve the edge of the foam; this will help to create a rounded posy shape.

2. Soak the foam (see Techniques) then secure it into the plastic dish using pot tape; the tape should reach completely around the dish and foam, overlapping at the ends to ensure a secure fixing. Then wedge the dish firmly into the teacup, using floral fix to do this if needed.

3. Insert a small selection of the leaves into the edge of the foam, following the edge of the cup.

4. Choose the best pink rose as your focal flower and place it in the centre of the foam, leaving approximately 8cm (3in) of stem showing. Then place the other three pink roses around it; these should be a little shorter in height and radiate out further. Fill the gaps with spray roses and astrantia.

5. Add the final leaves, trailing the berries of the leycesteria down the side of the teacup. Position the itea virginica and clematis near the focal rose and then drape the trails over the design to add movement.

6. Finally, gently tease out the tillandsia moss and tuck it into the flowers and foliage to add a wispy effect, then mist with water. Tie a ribbon bow around the teacup handle to enhance the design.

LEVEL 2   fresh or artificial   approx. 45 mins

Lighting the Way

This posy design displayed within a lantern looks wonderful hanging in a summer garden. Add battery-operated tea lights to light the way as darkness falls.

DESIGNED BY TINA PARKES

Ingredients

Flowers
- 4 white roses (A)
- 3 to 4 white lathyrus (sweet pea) (B)
- 3 white astilbe (C)
- a handful of tillandsia moss (D)

Sundries
- 1 square white lantern
- ⅓ block of floral foam
- 1 small shallow plastic dish to fit inside the lantern
- white fine gravel or sand
- 10 small wooden stars
- 2 to 3cm (¾ to 1¼in) of floral fix
- pot tape

Optional extra
- Long spouted watering can
- 2m (2yd) of ribbon

Recipe

1. Cut the floral foam to fit the small plastic dish, then use pot tape to secure the foam into the dish. Ensure the tape reaches completely around the dish and foam, overlapping the ends for a secure fixing.

2. Ensuring you keep the posy small enough to fit into the lantern, place your best rose in the centre of your design, cut to reach about two-thirds of the way up the lantern. Take time to get the placing right; if it is too tall or too short it won't be seen.

3. Place the remaining three roses around the central rose; they should be equally spaced, reach a little shorter and radiate out slightly further than the central rose.

4. Cut and add the sweet peas and astilbe to fill in the posy shape, then fill in the gaps with tillandsia moss and scatter the wooden stars into the design to finish your posy.

5. Attach some floral fix to the base of the dish and gently place the posy into the lantern, adding extra tillandsia moss or sand around the base (using a long spouted watering can if needed) to ensure that the plastic dish is not showing. Alternatively, place ribbon bows around the base of the dish to decorate.

LEVEL 2 fresh or artificial ⏱ approx. 40 mins

Orchid Heart

These dainty orchid hearts are perfect for decorating the backs of chairs; they will add detail to any corner that needs a special splash of colour.

DESIGNED BY DONNA CANN

Ingredients

Flowers
- 3 heads of phalaenopsis orchids (A)
- 1 stem of dendrobium orchids (B)
- 2 trails of clematis (C)

Sundries
- ⅙ block of floral foam
- 1 white wicker heart
- 1m (1yd) of violet ribbon
- pink bullion wire
- clear glue

Recipe

1. Start by pulling one end of the violet ribbon through the top of the wicker heart so you have two ends of even length by which to hang the design.

2. Cut a small piece of dry floral foam to wedge snugly into the recessed centre of the heart; this should be slightly lower than the surface to avoid it being seen. Once in position, lightly spray the foam with water.

3. Cut the phalaenopsis orchids and push them through the heart and foam to form a group of three flower heads in the centre of the design. By using three flower heads, this maintains a circular design; with four, it becomes square.

4. Follow by attaching the clematis stems into the foam, weaving the trails through the heart so that some hang long, then glue the dendrobium orchid heads around the edge of the heart.

5. Finally, seal the stems of two or three dendrobium orchid buds with glue. Wrap bullion wire tightly around the stems and twist to secure, then fix the wires to the bottom of the heart and hang them down with the clematis trails.

{ **make it chic**
Phalaenopsis orchids can be very sensitive to the gas released from ripe fruit and flowers; if your orchids do wilt, they can be revived by floating them in water. }

LEVEL 2   fresh or artificial   approx. 40 mins

In this level we explore a range of more challenging
techniques that will bring a wow factor to your design.

Ring of Roses

This enchanting, wreath-inspired design uses sumptuous blooms of varying shapes and sizes to create an almost fairy-tale effect.

DESIGNED BY CATHERINE DATE

Ingredients

Flowers
- 5 dark pink roses (A)
- 5 pale pink roses (B)
- 5 white bouvardia (C)
- 2 white eustoma (lisianthus) (D)
- 1 clematis trail (E)
- 5 pink astrantia (F)

Sundries
- 1 wired wreath ring
- clear sticky tape
- 1 A3 piece of strong white cardboard
- 1 roll of organza ribbon (colour of your choice)
- 10 glass test tubes
- wool (same colour as the ribbon)

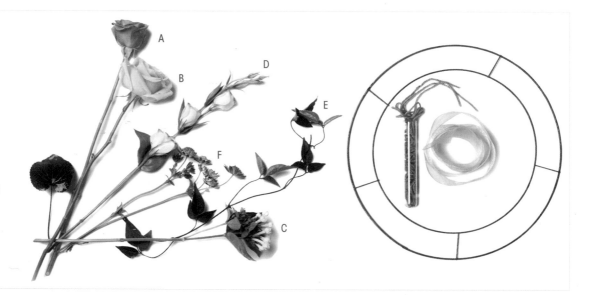

LEVEL 3   fresh or artificial   approx. 60 to 90 mins

Recipe

1. First, cut away the inner centre of the wire wreath ring so that you are left with a strong, single wire circle.

2. Cut the piece of cardboard to a width of 16cm (6in) then fold the cardboard in half for extra strength; its width should now measure 8cm (3in). Make sure you have enough cardboard length to reach around the ring; if not, simply join some additional card together.

3. Position the card around the outer edge of the ring and secure it in place using sticky tape. Neatly wind the ribbon around the cardboard frame so that it fully conceals it.

4. Secure the test tubes to the frame with wool then fill them with water.

5. Cut the flowers so their heads reach the top of the test tubes, then place a cluster of flowers in each tube.

6. Link these clusters by inserting the clematis stem in the test tube and gently draping it around the ring of flowers, securing it by inserting the other end in another test tube.

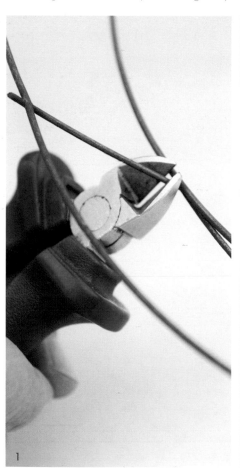

1

3

4

Summer Bouquet

This popular hand-tied design can be carried by a bride or used on a bridal table.
The floating grasses enhance the beautiful combinations of colour and texture.

DESIGNED BY CATHERINE DATE

Ingredients

Flowers
- 8 pink roses (A)
- 2 spray roses (B)
- 4 anethum (dill) (C)
- 20 stems of flexible vine
  e.g. mile-a-minute (D)
- 1 stem of astrantia (E)
- 10 stems of panicum
  virgatum (fountain grass)

Sundries
- 1 glass cube vase
- 1m (1yd) of ribbon
- 4 thick wires

Optional extra
- 5 white nigella

LEVEL 3   fresh or artificial   approx. 40 mins

Recipe

1. Strip the vine stems of leaves and bend them into a ring measuring approximately 25cm (10in) in diameter.

2. Secure the vine ring by winding further vine stems around it and tucking the ends into the frame.

3. Hook the four wires into the vine frame and bring them together to create a handle that will support the frame.

4. Start by inserting the flowers in groups into the circular frame, ensuring that the stems meet neatly as a spiral, until the frame is full (see Spiralling Stems). Then add the grasses to the outside of the frame, ensuring the stems sit comfortably within the existing spiral. Tie the design with string to secure.

5. Cut the stems so that the flower heads sit on the rim of the vase, then decorate the tie point with ribbon. Add water to the vase so that it does not cover the ribbon.

{ **make it unique**
If you wish, add nigella to the arrangement for additional texture. }

Along the Fence

This rustic design uses the countryside hedgerow as inspiration, combining rich hues and woody textures to evoke warm autumn days and an abundant harvest.

DESIGNED BY CATHERINE DATE

Ingredients

Flowers
- 4 burgundy dahlia (A)
- 2 red or pink bouvardia (B)
- 2 green hydrangea (C)
- 4 red roses (D)
- 4 stems of rubus vine (E)
- 10 malus (crab apples) (F)
- 10 stems of red cornus
- a few handfuls of moss

Sundries
- 1 block of floral foam
- 1 biodegradable spray tray
- 1 reel of red metallic wire
- 10 cocktail sticks (toothpicks)
- thick wire
- string

LEVEL 3   fresh or artificial   approx. 50 mins

Recipe

1. Soak a block of floral foam (see Techniques), then cut it to fit the tray. Secure the foam and the tray together by wrapping them with string.

2. Cut the cornus stems into short lengths and bundle them together in groups with the red wire. Secure these bundles upright along the edge of the foam using thick wire that has been shaped into hairpins.

3. Cover the rest of the foam with moss, again securing with wire pins. Infill with groups of flowers pushed into the foam along the top and rubus vine leaves inserted around the edge.

4. Inset a cocktail stick into the each crab apple. Push them into the foam to recess them evenly around the arrangement, adding colour and interest to the design

5. Finish by securing the rubus vine around the edge to add movement to the design and mist spray the design to keep it fresh.

2

{ **make it unique** }
Replace some of the flowers with decorative candles or baubles to create a festive finish.

Square within a Square

This geometric design is a real show-stopper. The contrast between the lush green of the foliage and the natural colour and irregular shape of the slate base makes for a dynamic centrepiece.

DESIGNED BY TINA PARKES

Ingredients

Flowers
- 3 bunches of myrtus communis (myrtle) (A)
- 2 green hydrangea (B)
- 4 berry clusters e.g phytolacca (C)
- 4 spray roses (D)

Sundries
- 1 block of floral foam
- 1 piece of slate
- 6 floral frogs
- floral fix
- silver stars on wires
- glue dots
- thick wire

Recipe

1. Cut a block of soaked floral foam in half longways to create a square. Using floral fix, attach the frogs to the slate (see Techniques) and place the foam on top.

2. Cut the myrtle into short pieces and starting from the bottom work upwards, inserting the myrtle stems closely together to cover the foam. Continue up the sides and over the top of the block until you are 3cm (a little over 1in) in from the outside edge and a square space is left in the centre of the foam.

3. Insert the hydrangea heads tightly into the foam to fill the internal square; you may need to pin the stems if they are weak.

4. Using wire, pin the lengths of berries along the edge of the internal square, then insert the roses. Using glue dots, attach stars to wire and place them into the design in a random pattern.

{ **make it chic** }
If you are using fresh flowers, water the design over a basin as there is no container to hold the water.

LEVEL 3   fresh or artificial approx. 90 mins

Calla Romanesque

The tall candlesticks used in this design evoke the classical columns
of Roman architecture, meanwhile the leaves that cover the spheres
and the hanging garlands further enhance the Roman theme.

DESIGNED BY DONNA CANN

Ingredients

Flowers
- 10 stems of cotinus (A)
- 7 zantedeschia (calla lilies) (B)
- 6 trails of jasmine

Sundries
- 3 tall candlesticks
- 2 x 12cm (4¾in) floral foam spheres
- 16cm (6¼in) floral foam sphere
- 3 floral pin holders
- floral fix
- thick wire

Recipe

1. Lightly soak all the floral foam spheres.

2. Now place floral fix on top of the candlesticks and secure a floral pin holder on top of each.

3. Starting at the bottom of each sphere, pin on the cotinus leaves and continue until the sphere is covered. Then secure the spheres on to the floral pin holders.

4. Use your thumb to bend the stems of the calla lilies to create a gentle curve (see Crisscross callas). Insert the calla lilies between the leaves at the top of each sphere so that they curve down the round edge, then secure with wire.

5. Finally, add the jasmine trails along the length of each lily to enhance the lines.

{ **make it chic** }
*Add a splash of colour by
substituting the calla lillies with tulips.*

LEVEL 3   fresh or artificial   approx. 2 hours

Hearts and Flowers

What could be more romantic than a heart covered with flowers and candles? Flowers in pastel shades complement the pretty theme to create a truly gorgeous piece that will grace any setting.

DESIGNED BY DONNA CANN

Ingredients

Flowers
- 5 blue or pink hydrangea (A)
- 5 aspidistra leaves (B)

Sundries
- 43cm (17in) diameter open heart floral foam frame
- white wool
- 6 glass tea light holders with picks
- 6 tea light candles
- pins

Recipe

1. Soak the floral foam frame (see Techniques).

2. Partly cover the floral foam frame with aspidistra leaves, secure them in place with pins, then decorate the frame by wrapping it with wool.

3. Ensuring the hydrangeas have been well conditioned, finish the design by cutting the florets from the stems and pushing them into the foam to create an even finish.

4. Nestle the candles by pushing their picks into the foam frame in groups of three.

5. Mist spray the design to keep it fresh.

{ **make it chic** }
Change the colourways of the design by using red hydrangea and autumn leaves.

LEVEL 3  fresh or artificial approx. 1 hour

Horizontal Blaze

This amazing design uses decorative sticks as a framework on which to build a display of beautiful blue scabiosa. Elegant amaranthus and ivy tendrils bind the arrangement together to create a truly striking finish.

DESIGNED BY DONNA CANN

Ingredients

Flowers
- 15 scabiosa (A)
- 8 amaranthus (B)
- 8 trails of ivy (C)
- a handful of moss (D)

Sundries
- 1 tall ceramic vase
- 1 bunch of white decorative sticks
- 1 block of floral foam
- white reel wire or string
- thick wire

LEVEL 3   fresh or artificial   approx. 1 hour

Recipe

1. Position the soaked foam upright in the vase so that it reaches approximately 5cm (2in) above the rim and is firmly wedged.

2. Lay out the decorative sticks to gauge their sizes, then insert several of the shorter ones into the foam at a horizontal angle.

3. Continue by overlaying the rest of the sticks on top of this framework.

2

4. Using the white reel wire or string, bind the sticks securely together in several places. For added security, fold the heavy wires into hairpin shapes and push these into the foam to firmly anchor the sticks.

5. Push the ivy into the foam and weave the trails among the sticks. Next position the scabiosa into the foam; these are the focal flowers, so scatter them evenly throughout the design with a denser grouping in the central area. Then work in the amaranthus so that some of the flowers hang underneath the design, and some are draping over the top to link all the materials.

6. To finish, cover any exposed foam with moss to hide it and secure where needed with wire hairpins made from thick wire.

3

{ **make it unique** }
Use driftwood instead of white sticks to bring a feel of the beach to your design.

Festive Ring

This lavish design with twinkling lights will add a touch of romance to a party, a wedding or a Christmas setting. Tightly pack the hydrangea so gaps don't appear as they dry and shrink and the design should last for months.

DESIGNED BY TINA PARKES

Ingredients

Flowers
- 5 red spray roses (A)
- 3 green hydrangea (B)
- 10 stems of rubus tricolor (C)
- 2 malus (crab apples) (D)
- 5 stems of piper nigrum (green peppercorns) (E)

Sundries
- 30cm (12in) diameter floral foam wreath ring
- 1 bag of potpourri
- 4 tea light holders
- 4 tea lights or candles
- 4 plastic floral frogs
- 8cm (3in) of floral fix
- stapler and staples
- cocktail sticks (toothpicks)
- wire

Recipe

1. Trim the edge of the floral foam wreath ring to soften the curve, then soak it.

2. Remove the rubus leaves from their stems, discarding any that are badly damaged. With the white-silver undersides on top, twist the leaves into cone shapes by folding in the outside edges, then fix them in position using a stapler.

3. Insert a first layer of rolled leaf stems at the bottom of the wreath frame to cover the base. Continue to add a second layer and even a third on top if you have enough leaves.

4. Attach a frog to the bottom of each tea light holder with some floral fix; insert the holders into the foam at equal distances apart then add the candles.

5. Start to add the hydrangea to the wreath, working from the inside out. Try to place the hydrangea compactly to create a cushioned look and ensure you push the stems into the foam to enable the flowers to drink.

6. Decorate the outside edge by inserting the spray roses in a random pattern. Insert half a cocktail stick into each crab apple and push into the foam. Finally add the green peppercorns and potpourri pieces, using wire if needed to secure.

{ **make it chic** }
Tall candles will bring an extra elegance to the design.

LEVEL 3   fresh or artificial approx. 1 hour

Eye-catching Elegance

Inspired by a garden water feature, this design uses the fresh colours of white and green to provide a crisp structure and the crocosmia leaves and meadow grasses to produce beautiful movement like wind near water.

DESIGNED BY CATHERINE DATE

Ingredients

Flowers
- 5 white roses (A)
- 3 white eustoma (lisianthus) (B)
- 5 nigella (C)
- 4 astilbe (D)
- a handful of meadow grasses (E)
- 10 crocosmia leaves

Sundries
- ½ block of floral foam
- cellophane and sticky tape
- glue dots
- green ribbon
- grey square flat dish
- white pebbles
- large elastic bands
- pins

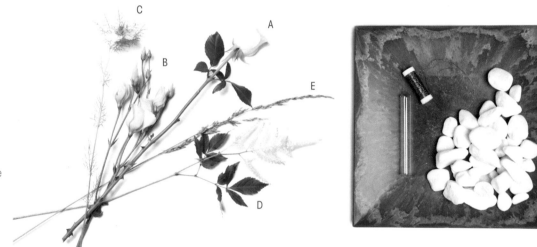

LEVEL 3   fresh or artificial   approx. 1 hour

Recipe

1. To prepare the container, soak the floral foam and cut it into an oval shape, then wrap it in cellophane so it does not leak (see Techniques).

2. Pin the crocosmia leaves around the outer edge of the cellophane, inserting the pins at the top of the cellophane to prevent any leakage.

3. Insert the meadow grasses into the foam; they will need to stand above the flowers as this will enlarge the design and add movement.

4. Fill in the design with flowers: add the roses first as the focal flowers, then the lisianthus, followed by the nigella and finally the astilbe.

5. Cover the edge of the design with green ribbon so that no leaves or cellophane are showing, using a few glue dots to secure. Finally, add a couple of pebbles on the flat dish to provide detail and visual weight.

{ **make it chic** }

Repeat this design on a windowsill to create an impactful display.

Myrtle Hedgerow

This luscious hedge-shaped design is ideal as a gift or as a display for a low coffee table where guests can look down on it. It makes an excellent arrangement for the Christmas vacation owing to its lasting qualities if kept moist.

DESIGNED BY TINA PARKES, INSPIRED BY GREGOR LERSCH

Ingredients

Flowers
- 5 bunches of myrtus communis (myrtle) (A)
- 5 cerise bouvardia (B)
- 1 box of redcurrants (C)

Sundries
- 1 square slate tile
- 1 tray to sit on slate
- 1 block of floral foam
- clear glue
- gold stars
- pot tape
- fine wire

Optional extra
- candles to decorate

Recipe

1. Soak the floral foam (see Techniques) and cut to fit the tray, then secure the foam firmly into the tray with pot tape.

2. Cut the myrtle into small pieces with short, chunky green tops, then remove the leaves from the bottom of the stems so they will insert cleanly into the foam.

3. Start to position the myrtle at one end of the foam and work your way along the length to create a dense hedge-like coverage.

4. Now insert the bouvardia down the centre of the design to add volume and colour, then drape the redcurrants around it to create movement, pinning with fine wire for added security if required.

5. As the finishing touch, glue the gold stars on top. Display the design on the slate tile with candles to decorate, if desired.

{ make it unique }

If kept moist this design will last a long time. You may wish to remove the red decorations and add a few buttons and beads for a fresh look.

LEVEL 3   fresh or artificial   approx. 1 hour

On the Champagne Trail

This elegant, beautiful design will grace any dining table and is perfect for celebrating that special occasion.

DESIGNED BY JULIE COLLINS

Ingredients

Flowers
- 10 roses (A)
- 5 astilbe (B)
- 10 amaranthus (C)
- 10 trails of clematis (D)
- 10 stems of rubus tricolor (E)

Sundries
- 1 tall cocktail vase
- 1 plastic container to fit inside the vase
- 1/3 block of floral foam
- pot tape
- glue dots
- decorative crushed glass or nuggets

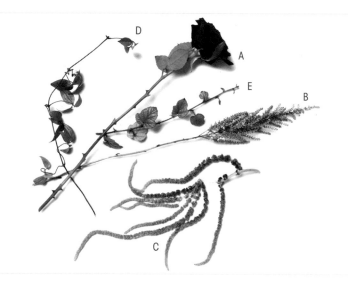

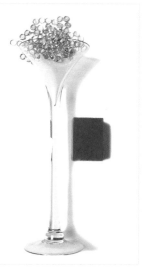

Recipe

1. Place the crushed glass into the bottom of the vase and nestle the container on top, making a well in the glass.

2. Soak the floral foam (see Techniques) and secure this into the plastic container using pot tape; reposition the container in the well on top of the crushed glass, ensuring it is secure with glue dots.

3. Insert rubus and clematis trails over the edge of the vase, keeping a few aside to add to the design at the end.

4. Now place the best rose in the centre of the foam, then position three more roses around the first; they should reach a little shorter and radiate out slightly further than the central one. Continue adding roses in this way, keeping the blooms close to the foam.

5. Finally add the amaranthus with some tucked under and some hanging over the other materials. Fill in with astilbe and place the last of the clematis and rubus over the top of the flowers to link it all together.

LEVEL 3   fresh or artificial   approx. 1 hour

Woodland Tranquility

This design evokes tranquil moments spent in shady woodland glades.
Its horizontal, textural qualities provide it with its natural appeal.

DESIGNED BY DONNA CANN

Ingredients

Flowers
- 10 white roses (A)
- 2 hydrangea (B)
- 5 astrantia (C)
- 6 trails of jasmine (D)
- 5 conifer branches (E)
- a handful of moss

Sundries
- 1 triple spray tray
- 3 blocks of floral foam
- paper-covered wire
- bark
- pot tape

LEVEL 3   fresh or artificial approx. 1 hour

Recipe

1. Soak the three blocks of floral foam (see Techniques), then trim off the edges to form curves. Secure the foam into the triple spray tray with pot tape, making sure that the tape reaches completely around the container and foam so the ends overlap.

2. Tie the bark to the side of the tray with the paper-covered wire, using some extra pieces to help cover the foam if needed. The more the foam is covered with bark, the less flower and foliage will be needed to finish the design.

3. Now establish the placement of the ten roses, which will be your focal flowers. Try laying them in the gaps between the bark along the length of the tray in groups of two or three. Once you achieve a balanced appearance, cut them and position them in the foam.

4. Add some of the jasmine trails, then fill in with some of the foliage and hydrangea heads to cover the foam and any exposed wires, working the materials into the design in groups.

5. Accent the roses by adding the astrantia around them to lift their colour, then add the last of the jasmine trails over the top to emphasize the horizontal movement of the design. To finish, fill any gaps with moss.

{ **make it chic**
This design looks best if you keep your materials cut low, following the horizontal form of the bark. }

Wild Twigs

This clever design uses twigs on the outside of the vase as well as within to add height and to support the flowers so you don't need so many. Combined together, the flowers and twigs create a lovely rustic texture and the lights add a special touch of fairy magic.

DESIGNED BY AMANDA RANDELL

Ingredients

Flowers
· 4 burgundy spray roses (A)
· 4 orange gerbera (B)
· 4 red hypericum (C)
· 4 orange crocosmia (D)

Sundries
· 2 bunches of birch twigs
· 1 tall vase
· battery-operated fairy lights
· reel wire
· pot tape

LEVEL 3   fresh or artificial   approx. 1 hour

Recipe

1. Start by laying out one bunch of birch twigs on the table. These need to reach to double the height of the vase, so measure one of the twigs against the vase to establish the correct height, then cut the whole bunch to size.

2. In order to start binding the twigs together, cut a long length of reel wire and place the first twig in the fold of the wire; twist the wire around it to secure.

3. In the same way, continue adding twigs to the wire until you have enough to wrap around the vase, then twist the ends of the wire together to secure them in place around the vase.

4. Wrap another length of wire around the bottom of the vase to secure the ends of the twigs as additional support.

5. Now insert the second bunch of twigs into the vase. Position the fairy lights in the twigs above the vase and tape the battery box to a firm twig.

6. Place the flowers in the vase, using the twigs to support them. Start by adding the gerbera as these have the greatest impact, then add the spray roses, the hypericum and finally the crocosmia.

7. To finish, fill the vase with water.

{ **make it chic** }
The design looks bolder if you group all the flowers together.

This section is designed to help you with some of the
important techniques mentioned in the book.

Equipment

You don't need to spend a fortune on floristry equipment. For a simple starter kit we would recommend a sturdy pair of floristry scissors, a small sharp knife and a pair of secateurs for cutting thicker stems. For a more advanced floristry kit, that is needed to make all the designs in this book, you will need the following:

Stapler: Used in floristry to secure certain items, particularly leaves when rolling them.

Reel wire: Useful for binding stems together.

Coloured reel wire: A decorative wire on a reel, available in a wide range of colours.

Pot tape: A strong fabric, sticky tape that is used to secure foam into a container.

Wire cutter: Used for cutting thicker wires.

Pins: Strong steel pins are used for securing and for decoration.

Paper-covered wire: Available in green or brown, ideal for binding stems together. The paper coating prevents the wire from slipping.

Test tubes: Available in plastic or glass, these can be used as a water source for the flowers.

Bullion wire: This decorative, crinkled wire comes in a range of colours.

Floral pin holder: Available in a range of sizes, this consists of a weighted round base with pins imbedded in.

Secateurs: Ideal for cutting thick or woody stems.

Glue dots: These small dots of tacky glue are used for sticking and securing. They work well on most dry surfaces.

Floral frog: A round plastic disk with four prongs used with floral fix to stop foam moving inside a container.

Floral fix: This is like a sticky green adhesive modelling clay, which is often used with a floral frog but can also hold wood and bark. Use on dry surfaces and with care, as it is not easily removed.

Small knife: Used for cutting stems and floral foam. Always keep it clean and sharp.

Scissors: Strong, with a short blade and blunt end, these are used for cutting stems.

115

Selecting Containers

Throughout this book, suggestions are provided in the sundry lists for containers to complement that particular design. As we have used a large range of containers, we hope you will be able to find something suitable. However here are a few guidelines for selecting your own container:

- First, ensure your container is waterproof; if in any doubt, line it with cellophane or insert a smaller waterproof container into it. Also ensure the container is stable so it won't fall over, and is clean before you start.

- If using floral foam with glass containers, you will need to consider how you cover the foam to avoid it being seen. This could be by using sand, gravel, sisal or even a leaf wrapped around the foam.

- The deeper the container is, the more floral foam or water it can hold. This is an important consideration, as using a deeper container will reduce the amount of times you will need to water the design after you have made it.

- Wherever possible, select a shape that will enhance your design. So if you are creating a round design then use a round container; likewise, if you are creating a square design then use a square container.

- As you shop, it is fun to keep an eye out for interesting containers or items that could be adapted into containers for your designs. For example, in the designs in this book we have used items such as a bucket, a tin can, test tubes and slate.

- Some floristry products have the oasis already set into the frame, for example this open heart floral frame.

make it chic

Terracotta pots and tin pails instantly add a touch of shabby chic. A tin can covered with an aspidistra leaf also makes a stunning container. Look out for interesting frames, such as this heart, which already has the floral foam inserted.

Soaking Floral Foam

It is vital to soak floral foam correctly to ensure your design lasts as long as possible. Modern floral foam does not take long to soak so you can prepare it as you need it. You will find that some floral foam products include flower food, which further extends the life of your designs.

Technique

1. To soak the foam effectively, use a container that is a little larger than the block of foam you wish to soak. Fill the container with cold water so that you will be able to fully submerge the foam.

2. Place the foam on the top of the water, then release it so that it starts to sink down.

3. It will take approximately two minutes for the foam to absorb the water and to gently sink just below the surface. Once the foam is soaked it is ready to be used in your design.

Wrapping Foam in Cellophane

This is a great way of making your own container if you don't have something suitable or would like to work with a specific colour scheme. If you are working to a budget, you could always recycle the cellophane in which the flowers were bought instead of buying fresh sheets.

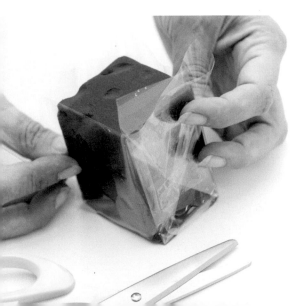

Technique

1. To wrap soaked floral foam, take a piece of cellophane and cut it to approximately twice the size of the foam.

2. Place the foam in the centre of the cellophane and fold up the edges as if you were wrapping a parcel. Then tape the ends to secure the cellophane in place around the foam.

3. Once wrapped, trim off any excess so that about 1cm (¼in) of cellophane is left above the top of the foam. This will prevent water splashing over the edge of the container when watering.

{ **make it chic**
Once the foam is wrapped in cellophane, it can be covered in hay, leaves, fabric, or whichever covering best suits your design. }

Preparing Flowers and Foliage

To keep your finished designs in top condition, the most important thing to remember is to place your cut stems in water as quickly as you can. However, there are some additional conditioning techniques that will help to ensure your designs last for as long as possible. Remember that some flowers require specialist care, so if in doubt please consult your florist or refer to the instructions that come with them.

Technique

1.   Take one or more clean buckets, fill them with 15 to 20cm (6 to 8in) of fresh, tepid water, then add flower food following the instructions on the packet.

2.   Remove any packaging from your flowers and foliage, then strip any foliage that will sit below the water line. Note that flowers that have travelled may feel soft but they will firm up after proper conditioning.

3.   Cut the ends of each stem with a pair of clean, sharp scissors or a knife at a 45-degree angle to allow effective hydration, then place immediately in the water. Be careful not to overfill the buckets with flowers.

4.   Remove thorns from roses with a small knife. If they are wilting, revive them by cutting the stems, wrapping the heads in paper to protect them, and placing the stem in 2.5cm (1in) of hot water for one minute before moving them back into tepid deep water.

5.   Keep your flowers in your cool location for at least 5 to 6 hours to allow the flowers to have a good drink. Keep any fruit separately as it releases ethylene gas, which promotes premature flower opening.

Buying flowers

Look for good quality flowers, which have crisp petals and foliage with no sign of damage. Flowers should be firm and not completely open. On linear flower forms, such as delphinium and gladioli blooms, the bottom flowers should be open and there should be colour on the lower buds.

Stems should be firm with no discolouration. Leaves should be free from damage and have no signs of pest or disease. Each flower should be checked to make sure there are no signs of Botrytis, which is a grey mold that will spread to other flowers and reduce their life. When handling flowers, no petals should fall off.

Making Hay Containers

Hay or straw containers add a gorgeously rustic feel to any design; moreover, they are surprisingly simple and cost-effective to make yourself.

Technique

1. Soak your floral foam and wrap it in cellophane (see Wrapping foam in cellophane).
2. Lay a length of string on the table, then tease out a handful of hay and spread it along the length of the string.
3. Place the wrapped foam in the centre of the hay and, using the ends of the string, pull the hay up around the foam.
4. Ensure the foam is completely covered, then secure the hay by tying the ends of the string tightly together.
5. Trim the hay with scissors – top and bottom – to create a neat finish.
6. Over bind the string tightly with rope or raffia to create a decorative feature.

3

4

In this wonderfully summery design, straw has been wrapped around the foam base for a complementary finish.

Working with Artificial Flowers

Artificial flowers can make a useful alternative to their fresh counterparts, especially where it is essential that a design remains in top condition over a long period of time. Most of the designs in this book can be made with artificial flowers, so you have the option to replace some or all of the fresh materials as fits the look or purpose of your design.

Many artificial flowers and foliages have a very strong wire in the centre of the stem to support the flower, so you will need a good pair of wire cutters to cut them with. There are special floral foams available if you are using just artificial or dried flowers; these are usually grey or brown in colour and have a firmer consistency than the foam for fresh flowers, which keeps the stems firmly in place.

Spiralling Stems

You will need to learn this technique in order to assemble stems into a hand-tied bouquet. We recommend that you practice first using one type of flower; this will help you to get the feel for how the stems fit together. Once you are comfortable with spiralling a simple bouquet, you can start adding additional flowers and foliage.

Technique

1. First take the bloom that is the largest and is in the best condition; this will become your focal flower in the centre of the design. Where you hold the stem dictates the size of the bunch, so if you would like to create a smaller posy then you need to hold the stem nearer the head; for a larger bouquet hold the stem lower down. This point is called the tie point and will be where all the stems cross into a spiral and where you tie the bouquet.

2. To prepare your materials, remove all the foliage from below the tie point on each of your stems (see Preparing flowers and foliage). Doing this will help to prevent bacteria growing in the water, thus ensuring your bouquet lasts longer; it also keeps the tie point as slim as possible, making it easier to hold.

3. To start the bouquet, hold the stem of your focal flower at the tie point. Then add three or four additional stems, just a little lower than the focal flower and parallel to each other at this stage.

4. To create the spiral, slightly twist the stems you have in your hand. When you add your next flowers into the bouquet place them in at a slight diagonal, with their stems fitting into the slight 'V' created by the original stems in your hand.

1

3

4

5. Keep turning and adding flowers and foliage until you have created the size of bouquet you want.

6. Tie the stems firmly at the tie point. First cut a long length of florist tie or string and fold it in half, putting the loop over your thumb.

7. Next, wind the length of florist tie or string above your hand and around the back of the bouquet as shown.

8. Now bring the ends back through the loop that you made with your thumb.

9. Separate the ends, taking them around the bouquet in opposite directions.

10. Then tightly tie the ends of the florist tie or string together, so the stems cannot move.

11. Hold the bouquet upside down by the stems, then gently close the stems tightly together and cut them straight across. As a general rule, the size to which the bouquet is cut should be one-third stems to two-thirds bouquet.

12. Let the stems splay out in your hand and cut the middle ones shorter than the outside stems by about 2cm (¾in). Turn your bouquet up the right way and it should stand

Maintaining Designs

Properly condition your flowers (see Preparing flowers and foliage) and then follow these guidelines to ensure they last as long as possible:

- Once you have finished making your design, top up with water and mist spray every two to three days. It is important not to let the floral foam dry completely as it cannot be re-soaked.
- Wherever possible, keep designs in cool locations but not below 5°C (41°F).
- Some flowers will die before others so if you can, remove these from the design and replace them with fresh alternatives.
- For artifical flowers, sprays are available to help reduce dust sticking; alternatively a quick blast with a hair drier on a cool or low heat keeps them looking good.

Disposing with Designs

Eventually a fresh design will look tired, which means that it is time to dispose of it. Here are some tips for doing this:

- First remove the stems from the foam and place them in the compost or recycle bin.
- The floral foam cannot be reused once it has dried out, but it will make excellent drainage in your planted containers so keep it in a plastic bag until you need it.
- Wash the used container with bleach to kill any bacteria, then dry and store it for the next time you feel creative.

Left to right: Julie Collins, Donna Cann, Tina Parkes, Amanda Randell and Catherine Date enjoying tea and cake after an inspirational day of floral design.

Useful Contacts and Suppliers

UK

Academy of Floral Art
www.academyoffloralart.com

National Association of Flower Arrangement Societies (NAFAS) www.nafas.org.uk

Scottish Association of Flower Arrangement Societies (SAFAS) www.safas.org.uk

British Floristry Association (BFA)
www.britishfloristassociation.co.uk

Worldwide

World Association of Flower Arrangers (WAFA) *www.wafausa.org*

USA

American Institute of Floral Designers (AIFD)
http://aifd.org

Canada

Canadian Academy of Floral Art (CAFA)
www.cafachat.com

Australia

Australian Floral Art Association (AFAA)
www.ausfloralart.org

New Zealand

Floral Art Society of New Zealand (FASNZ)
www.fasnz.org.nz

Acknowledgments

All the team at D&C for your help and support.
Our amazing Photographer Julian Winslow, the lovely Keri Highland. Plus Jack Kirby from bangwallop.
Our wonderful film crew from Westaway Film, Will and his team.
Our fantastic flower wholesaler Darren Lakin from DL Flowers for all the flowers he provided.
Our fabulous sundry wholesaler Gerard Van Stein.
Amanda and Daniel Seale, for the use of your beautiful venue at Woodmanton.
Georgina Craig, for the use of your gorgeous kitchen in the DVD.
And both our families and all our fantastic friends for all their generous help and support during the creation of the book, DVD and the Academy of Floral Art.

About the Authors

Julie Collins Btec ND, ICSF, Cert Ed, MDPF (English Master)

I started my career in floristry in 1996. I love the way floristry can use both my skills in creativity and business management. Since training I have combined my passion for teaching with running my own successful corporate and wedding flower business. In 2008 I joined forces with Tina Parkes and launched the Academy of Floral Art which has been the most exciting journey yet. I am inspired by the new European design styles and sharing my passion with anyone who loves flowers.

Tina Parkes NDSF, Cert Ed, Dutch Master, CFD, AIFD, FBFA

My passion for floral materials started at a young age with my own section of my parents' allotment. My Mum reminds me of how I used to bring in bunches of grasses and arrange them around the house in vases. My passion has grown from there, along with a passion for education. Floristry has also opened up a world of travelling, including living in the Netherlands for two years and being part of the British floristry team to demonstrate in Boston, America. My most exciting journey started with my business partner Julie Collins in September 2008 with the creation of the Academy of Floral Art.

About the Contributors

Donna Cann MDPF (English Master)

I started in floristry fresh out of school at the age of 16 and my love for all things floral continues to grow. Competing is my real passion, the nerves and adrenaline seem to bring out the best of my creativity. This past year has been one of my best; working alongside Tina, Julie, Catherine and Amanda has been great fun and very inspiring. Also winning first place in a tree dressing competition held at Chicheley Hall with Tina and Julie was a massive highlight!!

Amanda Randell ICSF, MDPF (English Master)

I love the fact that flowers are my life's focus. They preoccupy me with their form and colour and I am delighted by their variety. Arranging them gives me purpose and I will happily bore anyone who cares to listen to me talk about them. I have two other passions, my husband and daughter who, incredibly, are caught up in my desire to learn more.

Catherine Date NDSF Cert Ed

The best thing about floristry is there is always something new to learn. Floristry techniques are continually evolving and there are always lots of new varieties of flowers coming on to the market. I started training in floristry at the tender age of 16. After many competition wins and completing my training to the highest level, I went on and achieved my teaching Cert Ed qualification. I then decided to work in London for some of the top designers and have now returned to the West Country. As well as my freelance teaching role, I also run my own successful wedding flower business.

Index

A DAVID & CHARLES BOOK
© F&W Media International, LTD 2013

David & Charles is an imprint of F&W Media
International, Ltd
Brunel House, Forde Close, Newton Abbot,
TQ12 4PU, UK

F&W Media International, Ltd is a subsidiary
of F+W Media, Inc
10151 Carver Road, Suite #200, Blue Ash,
OH 45242, USA

First published in the UK and USA in 2013

Text and designs copyright © Julie Collins and Tina Parkes 2013
Layout © F&W Media International, LTD 2013
photography © Julie Collins and Tina Parkes 2013

A catalogue record for this book is available from the British Library.

ISBN-13: 978-1-4463-0329-0 paperback
ISBN-10: 1-4463-0329-2 hardback

Printed in China by RR Donnelley
for F&W Media International, LTD
Brunel House, Forde Close, Newton Abbot,
TQ12 4PU, UK

10 9 8 7 6 5 4 3 2 1

Publisher Alison Myer
Craft Business Manager UK: Ame Verso
Junior Acquisitions Editor James Brooks
Project Editor Freya Dangerfield, Bethany Dymond
Designer Manager Sarah Clark
Senior Production Controller Kelly Smith
Photographers Julian Winslow, Keri Highland, Jack Kirby

F+W Media publishes high-quality books on a wide range of subjects. For more great book